SEALED WITH A KILL

A Shocking True Crime Love Story

Rod Kackley

Lyons Circle Publishing Inc.

"The dynamics of this relationship were destructive -- almost cancerous."

ASSISTANT KENT COUNTY, MICH. PROSECUTOR DAVID SCHIEBER

CHAPTER ONE

Gwen Graham was in love, and it showed. The woman who brazenly displayed the cigarette burn scars on her arms by wearing short-sleeved t-shirts and blouses whenever possible, had moved to Grand Rapids, Mich. from Texas to follow the newest love of her life.

Fran Shadden was ten years older than Gwen and tried to be a calming influence on the petite, twenty-four-year-old woman with reddish blonde hair, and a charming smile.

Most people's first impression of Gwen was that she was cute and innocent. Most people were wrong.

Gwen's love in life, aside from a parade of boys and girls, was her 450cc motorcycle. A crash on the bike nearly cost Gwen her life and did result in a pair of false teeth to replace her front teeth that were knocked out when she wiped out on her bike.

Gwen excited Fran, but at the same time, she scared the woman who had come to Grand Rapids to work with a church missionary group.

Fran's relationship with Gwen seemed to be such a violation of her religious beliefs, but Fran was able to rationalize it by convincing herself that she was leading the young woman to a better life.

Gwen tried several jobs after moving to Grand Rapids. None worked out. But both she and Fran were convinced a nursing home, Alpine Manor, would be a better place for her.

Many of the patients in the two-hundred-room retirement/nursing home suffered from Alzheimer's or some other organic brain disease. Some suffered from multiple sclerosis or severe arthritis. All required extensive nursing care.

Gwen had no experience woking with patients who suffered from multiple sclerosis or severe arthritis which afflicted many of the four-hundred patients at Alpine Manor. But her personality won over the woman who was tasked with filling openings on the nursing home staff which suffered from one of the highest turnover rates in Michigan, for its type of business.

Gwen was hired and proved not only to be a quick study, but she was a hard worker. Best of all, for many of her coworkers, she loved women. And the women who worked at Alpine Manor loved Gwen.

In many ways, Catherine May Wood, 'Cathy,' to her friends and coworkers, was the polar opposite of Alpine Manor's newest nurses' aide. Where Gwen was petite and often mistaken for a much younger woman, Cathy's husband, Ken, had thought the woman who would become his wife was a boy when he viewed her from the back on the night he picked her up for their first date.

Cathy weighed three-hundred-pounds with platinum blonde dyed hair at the top of her six-foot-tall, broad-shouldered frame when she met Gwen.

A year older than Gwen, Cathy's personality and appearance had changed dramatically in the past 18 months thanks to her employment at Alpine Manor.

Her job gave her a new-found confidence, or at least it seemed to, and like Gwen, women who worked with Cathy loved her. She would come to love them, too, or at least like them enough to take them to bed.

Cathy weighed more than four-hundred-pounds on her first day at Alpine Manor. She had spent several years sheltered in the young family's small home on the northwest side of Grand Rapids after giving birth. Her days revolved around a fascination with board games, crossword puzzles, and fast food.

Perhaps, her husband, Ken, who was no lightweight either, could have forced her to get out of Cathy's favorite, overstuffed, comfortable chair parked in front of the TV. He could have demanded that Cathy do at least some housework, take better care of their daughter, and eat a balanced meal.

But Ken was working double shifts, rolling up as much overtime as possible at a local General Motors factory and was often so tired when he got home that he just didn't have the energy to fight Cathy.

Despite appearances, Cathy was a dynamo with an incredibly high Alpha personality. Even though she would take her breaks alone for the first year of her employment at Alpine Manor, and refuse to eat lunch with anyone else at the table, Cathy ruled the Wood family in the house that they rented from her mother.

When the house was cleaned, it was Ken who ran the vacuum cleaner. When their daughter, Jamie, needed something, it was Ken who provided her assistance. He never had time to worry about cooking balanced meals.

"Jesus, Cathy," Ken said as he kicked the door closed, holding three bags of fast food, one in each hand and the third in his teeth.

The TV was blaring, their daughter, was on the floor doing her homework, while Cathy, surrounded by the empty food bags of her last few days' meals, worked on a crossword puzzle.

This place is a fucking mess, again, Ken thought.

Jamie, their daughter, glanced at her mother, whose concentration was locked on her crossword puzzle, and got up to grab the Taco Bell bag from between her father's teeth.

Jamie gave Ken a quick kiss on the cheek as he bent down to make it easier for her to grab the bag of tacos.

Ken straightened his back and stood as tall as his five-foot-eleven-inch frame would allow, trying to will Cathy to at least glance his way.

Ken could have said something, but as he did every night, he followed Jennifer into the kitchen and helped her put a couple of paper plates on the Formica-topped table that was just barely big enough for four people to sit down for an evening meal.

The size of the table, which rest unevenly on four legs, tottering on the warped kitchen floor, wouldn't be a concern this night. It never was.

Ken and Jamie would eat at the table after delivering a bag to the TV tray that Cathy used for meals at least three times daily.

Ken stopped for a moment and looked at his overweight wife again. He was hoping that maybe, just perhaps, Cathy would be able to struggle out of that damn chair just once to help him set the table for what would pass as the family's evening meal.

This night was like the last, and the night before. Ken brought home the fast food that Cathy wanted, along with a dinner in a paper bag for himself, and they gained weight together.

That isn't to say that Ken was a lap dog for Cathy. Their

relationship was by turns contentious, stormy, and even violent. But she usually won.

Even when Cathy didn't come out on top, she would — as devotees of the BDSM lifestyle in which she was destined to find herself — top from the bottom.

Ken tried to get Cathy to be a better wife and mother.

But it seemed hopeless. It had been months since they had made love. Ken had stopped asking. It was easier to work split shifts at the GM plant, come home from a nine-hour shift long enough to throw some fast food in front of his wife and daughter, and then go back for another nine-hour shift.

"Hey, I'd rather pick up the O-T and be here than at home watching that fat pig eat herself to death," Ken said to a sympathetic coworker.

The lack of sex was one thing. Cathy had used Ken's libido to control him ever since their first date. Cathy understood better than anyone what scared and bothered Ken more than hardly ever getting any sex from her was his fear of losing her.

She tested him. From their first date, Cathy got her girlfriends to call Ken and flirt with him over the phone. They would call to see if they could get Ken to crack and come on to them.

But he didn't. Ken, for some reason, couldn't help but be devoted to Cathy.

Ken convinced himself that Cathy needed him and would die if he left.

So he compromised.

But Cathy's relationship with their daughter, Jamie, was another thing. The little girl was truly the apple of Ken's eye if only because she was the only living soul in their family who took the time and trouble to have a conversation with him.

Cathy had never been able to handle being a mother.

"Jamie is such a bully," she would say to Ken as Cathy tried to explain why she hadn't change the baby's diaper. "I can't stand to be around her."

If there was any doubt in Ken's mind about his wife's inability to be a mother, it was erased during an afternoon baseball game at Detroit Tiger's stadium.

Jamie was just a baby at the time, and Cathy still was small enough to at least squeeze into a seat at the ballpark.

They were sitting in the stands along the third-base side of the field when a foul ball, a line drive, came at them.

Cathy screamed. She held Jamie up in front of her face to protect herself.

Ken reached out and caught the ball with his bare hand.

CHAPTER TWO

Cathy spotted Gwen from across the employee cafeteria and was immediately attracted to the young woman who looked more like a girl. Many of Cathy's fellow female employees were as large as she.

So, Cathy's petite frame made her look like a model compared to the competition.

Cathy wanted Gwen, and what Cathy wanted, Cathy was accustomed to getting.

By the time Gwen started what would become a short career as a nurses' aide, Cathy had come to control Alpine Manor. She managed her fellow workers by alternating between playing the victim and the victor.

Cathy could cry as easily as the best TV soap actress. She was able to play on the softer emotions of her coworkers to get them to switch shifts with her, cover when Cathy decided she needed a break, and work with the more challenging patients.

Cathy could also use her acting ability to control her supervisors and the nurses who were supposed to be in charge of the staff. Actually, that wasn't much of a challenge. The supervisors at Alpine Manor were usually so overworked, they didn't put up much of a fight.

Still, there were those who resisted.

If one of the other nurses' aides didn't bend to Cathy's will, she wouldn't depend on her acting ability to win them over. Cathy would do things like pour water into the sheets of the patients of the aides who were on her hit list to make it look like they had not been doing their jobs.

Or Cathy would spread rumors about them; focusing on everything from their work performance to stories about cheating on their spouses. A couple of divorces on the nurses' aides staff were the result of rumors spread by Cathy.

Those who didn't fear Cathy or bow to her will were just dispensed with.

And then in walked Gwen.

To say it was love, at first sight, would be an overstatement. Love didn't have anything to do with Cathy's emotions that night on third shift. There was desire, that is true. But more than the raw lust that fueled Cathy's sex drive, her need for Gwen was the desire to have the young woman before, and more thoroughly, than anyone else.

It wasn't the first time Cathy had targeted a new woman on the Alpine Manor staff just because she could. But this time, Cathy had someone in her sites who would be more than a challenge; she would be the perfect match.

At least that's the way Cathy would tell the story.

Cathy didn't make an immediate play for Gwen, other than introducing herself to the new employee, making her welcome, and inviting her home for one of the after work parties that had become legendary at Alpine Manor.

By this time, Ken and Jamie had jumped off Cathy's emotional rollercoaster. It was Ken's decision. His wife had become violent. Their battles had turned physical.

Even with violence being part of the equation, it wasn't that he didn't want Cathy to be a part of Jamie's life. It wasn't even that he was afraid she would hurt Jamie. It was more that Cathy just didn't seem to want to be a part of her daughter's life.

She just didn't care.

However, he may have misjudged Cathy. Perhaps Ken should have been worried about the violence.

"I have a tendency when I get around children to be a child abuser," Cathy said. "I just want to slap them. I can't stand kids — even Jamie."

So, it was probably best for all involved that Ken and Jamie had fled. If nothing else it left Cathy free to explore the wilder side of her personality.

She began to throw wild, liquor and drug fueled, parties at her small northwest side Grand Rapids home. Neighbors complained about the loud music, the shouts and screams, and fights in the backyard of the home. They even reported naked or nearly naked people running through the streets.

Gwen was invited.

She was also invited to one of the local bars where Cathy organized after work socials that involved lesbians, like herself and Gwen, at one of Grand Rapids' gay bars.

There were a few women who hit on Gwen first. Some of them were even enticed by Cathy to approach the young lady from Texas. So even though Cathy might not have been first at the plate, she was controlling the lineup.

Before long, though, it was Cathy's turn.

And she and Gwen fell in love, deeply in love.

The sex was incredible and uninhibited by any kind of societal convention. They used dildos and other sex toys during their romps in the bed at Cathy's house. One night, with the windows wide open, Cathy's neighbors were treated to the sounds of, as one man explained to his wife, "Two women going at it."

The sex wasn't confined to Cathy's house. They did it

outdoors at night in the backyard, in the backseats of cars, even in storage closets and empty patient rooms at Alpine Manor.

But it was also much like the sweet teenage love affair of two virginal children.

Cathy and Gwen traded sappy, gushing love poems as testaments to their vows of undying love. They would test each other with games, they would have silly flirtations at the parties and bars with other women, and then dash outside to fall into each other's arms.

Cathy would also have women call Gwen, just like she had her girlfriends call Ken, to test Gwen's faithfulness.

But that wasn't enough.

The women — answering the question of who thought of it first depends on who is telling the story, Cathy or Gwen — devised the ultimate test of trust and faithfulness.

They were going to start killing Alpine Manor patients, pledging each other to secrecy, thereby creating a bond of blood that would cement their relationship.

Of course, they also came up with a rule that would help ensure neither talked. They agreed to share the murders.

So they would be mutually guilty and if nothing else, afraid to rat out the other for fear of being accused; Cathy would do a killing, then Gwen would do the next one.

Cathy and Gwen decided to kill only those who seemed closest to death for their game. That would serve two purposes.

First, if the patient would die soon anyway, what moral difference did it make if Cathy and Gwen sped up the inevitable by a few days or weeks.

Second, if the doctors on staff had already told everyone the patients would die soon, and of natural causes, who would bother investigating? It was a sad fact of life and death that when patients died at Alpine Manor autopsies were never performed as was the rule when a person died outside of a hospital.

A brief examination was conducted, a toe tag was applied, the coroner and the surviving family were notified, the corpse washed and cleaned, and the bed prepared for the next patient.

Other than deciding which patients were most likely to die, Cathy and Gwen created one more benchmark for their evil game. They decided to choose their victims so that the first initial of their names spelled the word, murder.

In January 1987, Cathy and Gwen went for the first kill.

CHAPTER THREE

Cathy and Gwen needed to do some research. Not only were they looking for patients whose names could be used to spell "murder" and patients who were most likely to die; they wanted patients who were easy to kill.

That required some experimentation. Cathy went from patient to patient, while Gwen kept watch at the door. Cathy would pinch the patient's nose and hold his or her mouth closed to see how much resistance they could offer.

One patient in particular fought back valiantly. Even though he didn't have much else going for him, the man's jaw muscles were just too strong for Cathy to hold closed. Too bad. His first name, Ulysses, would have given them the letter in the acronym of death that was proving to be the toughest to find.

Cathy and Gwen found the experimentation to be incredibly exciting and even erotic. Both were breathing heavily, as Gwen stood watch in the hall and Cathy lumbered up onto the patient.

When each experiment was over, beads of sweat would be visible on Cathy's brow as the girlfriends retired quickly to an empty room to bring each other to incredible orgasms.

Finally, after much deliberation, they chose their first victim, Marguerite Chambers.

It was January 1987 and time to go for the first kill, the

"M" of "murder."

They would take turns killing one patient after another. Cathy would do the first.

This was the night Marguerite Chambers was going to die.

Gwen watched the hallway outside the sixty-five-year-old woman's room, while Cathy crept as silently as possible into the room and stood beside Marguerite's bed. The old lady was sound asleep. Because she was a wanderer, Marguerite's wrists and ankles were encased in soft leather straps to keep her in bed.

Cathy looked down at her face. Marguerite was sleeping so soundly, so peacefully, it looked like she had already crossed over the River Jordan to a happier place.

But she had not. It was time to seal the lesbian love bond that Cathy and Gwen had been forging since the day they met.

Cathy got ready to pull herself onto the bed. The plan was to straddle Marguerite's fragile body and gently, but firmly, place a rolled up washcloth over her nose and mouth.

It was the most humane, yet efficient way that Gwen and Cathy had thought of to take the lives that they felt needed to end.

The patients who had a red target on their backs, as far as the lovers were concerned, were those who were ready to exit anyway. And often, they required so much medication to ease their pain, if they even knew where they were, that Gwen and Cathy could rationalize their murders as mercy killings.

Yet, Cathy froze.

She just couldn't do it.

Even though she ran Alpine Manor with an iron first and

was more than willing to ruthlessly ruin the marriages and careers of fellow employees who ran afoul of her and Gwen; Cathy couldn't do this.

She couldn't kill Marguerite Chambers. Maybe the next one could be hers, but not Marguerite. Not now. Not tonight.

Gwen was standing nervously outside Marguerite Chambers' room. She was twisting her hands and biting her lower lip. Gwen knew she couldn't afford to look nervous if anyone walked up to her, but that was much easier thought than done.

What if someone did come down the hall? What if a nurse or another aide wanted to do a nightly check on Marguerite? What if a supervisor should come by? How would Gwen explain why she was standing outside the room with a closed door? And why was the door shut? That was completely against Alpine Manor policy.

It didn't matter why Gwen was in the hallway. She was sure she could explain that away. But what would she do about a supervisor who decided to barge into the room to see what was going on?

Good God, Gwen thought. Just imagine the look on any of their faces if they walked in and found Cathy straddling over the body of this old lady with a rolled up washcloth pressed over her face.

What was taking so damn long? Cathy should have done it by now. What had gone wrong?

Gwen's fears were only exacerbated by the seconds ticking by like days as she waited for Cathy to finish off the old lady.

Finally, she couldn't take it anymore. Gwen opened the door a crack and peeked inside.

Oh for Christ's sake! Cathy was standing by Marguerite's

bed twisting the washcloth into a pretzel. She looked like she was going to pee her pants!

Cathy heard the soft whisper of the door opening, and saw Gwen looking inside the room. Cathy felt like a kid who had been caught doing something wrong.

Gwen closed the door, leaned back against the hallway wall, and rubbed her forehead. What now? She could tell Cathy was not going to be able to do this. That raised another question. If Cathy couldn't kill and Gwen had to do all the killings, what would that do to their love bond? What would that do to the policy of mutual destruction that was meant to keep the lovers from ratting each other out?

Gwen took a deep breath, looked up at the white ceiling tiles, gathered her thoughts and went into the room.

She didn't say a word. Gwen could see this mountain of a woman she loved more than life itself was trembling like building ready to collapse over the San Andreas fault.

And what if she did? If Cathy passed out and hit the ground, there was no way Gwen would be able to drag her out. Imagine the look on a supervisor's face if she came in and found little Gwen, trying to drag Cathy, who was twice her size, out by the ankles.

Gwen put out her hand. Cathy gave her the washcloth. Gwen jumped up on to Marguerite's bed and straddled the woman.

With her arms and legs bound to the bed, there was no way Marguerite could fight back. She wouldn't have stood a chance even if she hadn't been tied down. Gwen might have only been five-foot-two, but she was a fighter, a scrapper, and Gwen was as tightly muscled as an athlete.

She often helped over aides tussle with the most violent patients. Besides the scars left by her self-inflicted cigarette burns, Gwen's body carried the evidence of barroom battles and lovers' quarrels that had left their own marks.

It wasn't unusual for Gwen to volunteer to assist moving large beds and desks, or lifting obese patients into and out of bathtubs.

Killing Marguerite wasn't any harder than snuffing out the life of a fly.

The old lady's eyes flashed open in fright for a second. But they soon stared lifelessly at the ceiling.

The murder was done. It was the first. Cathy was in tears. Even though it hadn't required much physical exertion, Gwen was breathing heavily.

They smiled at each other. Cathy and Gwen felt that they shared an unbreakable bond.

They could wait to get their hands in each others' pants.

Gwen grabbed a trinket off Marguerite's night table as a souvenir and then dashed out of the room holding Cathy's hand, pulling her much larger lover into a storage closet.

Both would enjoy an intense, quick orgasm that would serve to take the edge off until they could get into the bed and celebrate more appropriately.

Cathy and Gwen had their "M." There were only five letters and patients to go.

CHAPTER FOUR

And on and on it went. One patient after another fell to Cathy and Gwen's gamesmanship.

They soon gave up the idea of spelling the word "murder." It was just too hard to find patients who were easy to kill, ready to die, and with names that started with the correct letters for their acronymic quest.

It didn't matter. Cathy and Gwen switched to a new goal. They now concentrated on killing the proper number of patients to fit Cathy's poem, that included the magic line, "Forever and five days."

It was decided they would kill five patients.

And for a few months in 1987, that is just what they did.

Marguerite Chambers was the first victim. She was sixty-five years old and had been diagnosed with Alzheimer's five years before. But her family was still surprised to hear of her death.

Myrtle Luce was the second victim. She was ninety-five and had suffered a series of strokes. She had been losing weight. The other nurses and aides were not surprised by her death.

Mae Mason was the third victim. She was seventy-nine. Cathy said she kept staff busy in another part of the building so Gwen could kill her.

Seventy-four-year-old Belle Burkhard was the fourth

victim. This death raised suspicions among the Alpine Manor staff. She was found dead with her arm bruised and twisted under her body. Cathy would say later that the arm was bruised when Gwen knelt on it as she suffocated the woman with a wash cloth.

Edith Cook was the fifth and final victim. She was ninety-seven, very ill, add was kept sedated. Cathy considered the murder of Edith Cook to be a true mercy killing.

Each kill was exciting, even erotic. Gwen had to do them all. After a while, they stopped pretending to share the murders. Cathy stood watch. Gwen killed.

Some of the old people went down harder than the others, but they all went down.

After the first couple of killings, Cathy and Gwen would tread cautiously around Alpine Manor, being so polite and respectful that their behavior nearly raised red flags.

It was such a 360-degree turn in attitude, especially for Cathy, that the supervisors and nurses, even the other aides noticed. But they were so busy -- most were working double shifts or at the very least seven days or nights a week -- that they were just glad to have a little less drama in their work lives.

Each day, though, Cathy and Gwen expected to be visited by a Grand Rapids homicide detective. What would they do if arrested? What would they say? Late at night when both were home, they would drink Jack Daniels and try to concoct a believable story.

Maybe they could implicate another employee like a hated aide or a nurse? That idea was offered and rejected.

Cathy felt the guilt bearing down on her. She opened up to Ken, often visiting her estranged husband, but only when she could be sure their daughter Jaime would not be at home.

Ken had always felt Cathy needed some kind of psychiatric help. Even when she was still in high school, her paranoid pranks of having her friends call and ask Ken out for a date to test his resolve became somewhat more than annoying.

He knew that Cathy and Gwen were living together in the home that he had shared with Cathy and Jaime when they were a family. Ken was also aware of the wild parties Cathy held at the house. Old friends and neighbors told him of people fighting, carousing, even running nearly naked or buck naked in the street.

Yet, there were times when he felt like they could get back together. Cathy would visit his apartment. She would actually speak to Jaime. After their daughter went to bed, Ken and Cathy would cuddle on a living room sofa. Once in a while they even had sex.

He had hope.

But there was also an evening when Ken had gone back to the house to rescue some record albums and other belongings. Gwen came out of the bedroom with her head down, walking by Ken as if he didn't exist. And for some reason, that lit Cathy's fuse.

She went into a violent tirade, accusing Ken of everything under the sun including cheating on her and stealing Jamie away from her.

Cathy pushed Ken, or maybe he shoved her first to get out of the house. The exact sequence of events in a domestic battle are often hard to remember. But what Ken was sure of was being knocked to the ground by Gwen, looking up, and seeing Cathy standing over him with a baseball bat.

My God, he thought, they are going to kill me.

Fortunately, this was one night when the neighbors called 911 to complain about the noise.

As Cathy pulled back and raised the bat over her shoulder, the voice of a GRPD officer stopped her by ordering her to drop the bat.

No charges were filed. Ken grabbed his belongings, and shaken to his core, went home.

A few days later, Cathy knocked at his apartment door only to collapse into his arms shaking with fear and guilt, mumbling something about some crime that Gwen had committed and how she was deathly afraid they would both go to prison and be doomed to hell.

Even after all that had happened, Ken was ready to take her back. And he told her so.

But if only to prove Ken's amateur diagnosis of Cathy's bipolar mental state was correct, a few days later when the two ran into each other, she was her old arrogant, pugnacious self.

Ken had no way of knowing, but Gwen and Cathy were feeling much better about their game. The deaths of old people are never a surprise at a nursing home. And if there are no marks or other signs of violence, the funeral home, and the families are called, and the dead are laid to rest.

The game was fun, again.

Cathy and Gwen kept killing.

But then came Robin, a new nurse's aide who would unknowingly put Cathy and Gwen's lesbian lovers bond to the ultimate test.

CHAPTER FIVE

Robin Fielder was fresh out of high school, a little on the plump side, but she was also very close to voluptuous. It was easy to see that she had the curves of a woman. She also had the desires of a woman, even though Robin never had a real boyfriend in high school.

She never met anyone she wanted in that way.

At Alpine Manor, Robin found Gwen.

As far as the younger, less experienced, virgin was concerned, they had a friendship. From Gwen's point of view, the relationship was destined to become much more than that.

With Gwen taking the lead in and out of bed, she and Robin became much more than just friends. The attention showered on the younger woman motivated Robin to take even better care of herself and to lose weight.

The womanly curves that were slightly hidden before came into full view. Now Robin was voluptuous.

Still, Robin wasn't ready to fully committed to her relationship with Gwen. After all, she had never had a boyfriend. She had never slept with a man. How was Robin to really know if going to bed with Gwen was love, lust, or just convenient?

Even though her time with Gwen was all fun and no commitment to Robin, she knew she was playing with fire.

Gwen was cheating on Cathy. Both women had promised

each other to never play with another unless they were open about it and asked permission.

Gwen had broken that promise. There were few among their circle of friends and coworkers who had not spent time in bed with the Texan. But this relationship with Robin was something else.

Cathy wanted the young girl as a notch on her bedpost. She couldn't have her. Gwen got her.

It was enough to ignite Cathy's simmering jealousy and fear of losing Gwen. At the same time, Gwen was growing tired of being dominated at home, and now at work, by Cathy. She was ready to break away.

Gwen's relationship with Fran, the woman she had followed from Texas to Grand Rapids, was, in essence, a mother-daughter affair. She had grown tiered of that, too.

Gwen sensed that is what Cathy wanted. She made Gwen wear her hair in the style of a child's pigtails. Cathy wanted to tell her how to dress, how to act.

Gwen was sick of it.

Their emotions soon exploded into violence.

Cathy and Gwen got into a slapping contest during a practice session for the Alpine Manor softball team.

Cathy was managing the team in her best Machiavellian manner.

"Do a pirouette for me, dear," she mocked one player who had muffed a ground ball, forcing the woman to stand on tiptoe, put her hands on her head, and turn circles at second base.

Gwen was taking the team much more seriously. She was the athlete that Cathy had never been.

"Run, damn it, run!" Gwen yelled at Cathy when her lover hit a ball into the outfield.

Cathy tossed her bat aside and walked to first base, not

even coming close to beating the right fielder's throw.

"You bitch," Gwen said, as she slapped Cathy across the face.

That's all it took to incite another Gwen-Cathy donnybrook.

Cathy jumped on Gwen, knocking the smaller woman to the ground. She pinned her arms to the dirt of the infield with her knees and used both fists to bash her lover's face.

Breathing slowly and deeply, Cathy finally stopped punching. She rested her hands on her thighs and looked down with contempt on the face of the girl to whom she had pledged her everlasting love.

Cathy spat in Gwen's face before getting to her feet and dragging Gwen off the field by her ponytail as Gwen pleaded for mercy.

The others, who at first were excited by the violence -- it certainly wasn't the first time they had seen Cathy and Gwen fight -- were as exhausted as Cathy. Most were also happy they weren't on the receiving end of Cathy's anger.

Gwen for her part, had had enough of Cathy and Alpine Manor. She gave notice and moved on to a better job. She was still in Grand Rapids, but at least, Gwen felt like she was moving on.

Robin had never seen anything like the fight on the ballfield before. Even though Robin had started drinking heavily, smoking pot, and playing with Gwen; she was a stranger to the kind of violence she had just witnessed.

Although she would have been hard pressed to imagine anything worse than what she had just seen, Robin became something of a participant in another fight that could have turned deadly.

She was with Gwen, driving her ChevyLuv pickup truck when they spotted Cathy.

Robin skidded to a stop. Cathy pulled Gwen out of the truck, threw her into the bed of the pickup and jumped on top of her.

The smaller woman was able to scramble away from Cathy after landing several punches to the larger woman's face.

Gwen jumped into the back of the pickup truck.

"Drive, damn it, drive!"

Robin reacted a second too slowly. In the few seconds, it took Robin to wonder if she really should accelerate away and leave Cathy bleeding on the pavement, Cathy was able to jump into the truck's bed.

Just as Cathy grabbed Gwen's throat, Robin punched the accelerator with her foot, and they were off.

Cathy and Gwen were actually fighting in the back of a Chevy pickup as Robin drove the truck through the streets of Grand Rapids.

"Faster, go faster," Cathy screamed at Robin through the open window between the truck's interior and the vehicle's bed.

Cathy punched and kicked Gwen in the bed of the truck. Gwen fought back and for a moment was able to get on top of her.

She was able to stand at one point but fell on top of the much stronger woman when Robin turned a corner.

Robin, for her part, was crying, deathly afraid not only of what was happening to Gwen but what might happen to her if Cathy won. Still, she drove on.

Cathy screamed again for Robin to drive faster as she punched and kicked Gwen.

Robin looked back in the mirror and saw that Gwen's blouse had been ripped and torn. Soon the shirt split completely, blew off Gwen's shivering body and flew away in the wind.

Cathy finally ordered Robin to stop the truck, and as it came to a halt, reached for Gwen's ponytail.

But Cathy wasn't able to keep her grip on Gwen's hair. The smaller woman punched straight up, ramming her knuckles into Cathy's jaw, and broke free.

Gwen jumped out of the truck and ran shirtless into a cemetery where she hid in some shrubs.

Cathy's blood lust far from satisfied. She and Robin split up to search for Gwen.

Luckily for Gwen, it was Robin who found her.

Both of Gwen's eyes were blackened, her nose was bleeding and swollen, and she used her arms to cover her bare breasts.

"Stay here," Robin whispered.

She knelt beside Gwen in the bushes and stroked her hair. Furtively, she glanced back over her shoulder for Cathy.

"Don't move," Robin said. "I'll come back to get you after I drive Cathy home."

Hoping Robin would be as good as her word, Gwen crept even further into the bushes, when she saw Robin talking to Cathy.

For a second, it looked like Cathy would walk right toward Gwen. But Robin was able to grab her right arm and pull the woman to a different path.

Robin returned an hour later, sans Cathy and helped Gwen limp to the truck.

Although she had survived the battle, Gwen was ready to surrender. Grand Rapids, Mich. just didn't look that good to her anymore.

Gwen made plans to leave for Texas the next month. She decided to take Robin with her.

CHAPTER SIX

Cathy was alone in her apartment. Gwen and Robin had become a couple and were talking about moving to Texas. The others at Alpine Manor didn't seem to care to join her for bawdy parties anymore, and truth be told, Cathy had grown tired of the life, too.

Cathy had only one person left that she felt like she could talk to. Or maybe he was the last person on Earth she could still control. Whatever the reason, she needed to talk. Cathy felt like she would explode if she didn't open up.

Cathy needed to talk to Ken.

However, Cathy wasn't ready to face him in person. She called him on the phone.

She started off by telling Ken about a time when she and Gwen had stolen a lawn mower. And then she talked about taking eggs.

Why is she telling me about a couple of petty crimes, he wondered. Ken was afraid this was just the beginning. There had to be more. He didn't want to know, but he felt that confession would be good for Cathy's soul. Whether it was because he felt he could really help her or just wanted to make himself feel good, Ken did want to help Cathy.

"What else did you guys do?"

"Promise you will never tell anybody?"

Ken literally shivered. He was afraid of what the answer would be. He knew how Cathy and Gwen could be when they were together.

"What did you do?"

"You can't tell anybody."

"Come on. I want an answer."

"You won't tell?"

"Never, I promise. I will never tell."

"What's the worst thing a person could do?"

My God, there it is, he thought. The opening Ken had been waiting for. He had to answer the question if only to rule out the possibility that his wife, the woman he had loved through everything, the mother of his child, was some kind of a homicidal maniac.

"Murder would be the worst. Killing someone would be the worst thing anyone could do."

Cathy's silence was his answer.

"Oh Lord Jesus, Cathy, you didn't."

"We did," Cathy said as Ken put his face in his hands.

"We did it six times."

Ken sat silently as Cathy told him all about the murders. She described how Gwen had climbed on top of each of the women she killed and suffocated the life out of them.

Ken didn't want to believe it. Why should he? Ken had known since her high school days that Cathy was a pathological liar. She never could help herself. She just told tales.

Cathy would create incredible fantasies in her mind and then spin them out into wild stories. Maybe she came to believe the lies that she created as part of her fantasy world. He wasn't sure, but Ken didn't have trouble understanding that.

The story she told early in their relationship about how as a young girl she was seduced by a teenage girl who raped her with a dildo was the first story Ken had trouble believing. But Cathy told it so well and apparently felt it was true, so Ken did too.

Still, this story of Gwen and Cathy conspiring to kill people at Alpine Manor was too much for Ken.

Think about what this poor guy had been through since the day he met Cathy. She got her friends to flirt with Ken to test his love and devotion. Then after getting married, Cathy decided she really was a lesbian, something that wasn't looked at the same way in 1987 the way it is now, especially in a town like Grand Rapids, Mich.

Cathy had abandoned him and their daughter, and now she was telling him that she and her girlfriend were serial killers.

So, he did what any husband would do in a similar situation, Ken took Cathy to Las Vegas for a vacation.

They would spend three days and nights in Sin City. How appropriate was that?

It was his way of finding out what Cathy had become. Was she the same woman he had married, or had she turned into a murderer? And if she was telling the truth, about doing the killings, was she still dangerous to him and more importantly to Jamie?

Nothing that happened in Vegas should have dissuaded Ken from the inevitable conclusion that his wife had at least helped to kill five people. Nor could he doubt now that she could kill again.

Or could he?

Cathy got drunk, loud and obnoxious in the casinos. She threatened to fight the dealers. She and Ken fought in their room and but then, not unlike what Cathy and Gwen would do, they made love.

Still, for the next year Ken kept telling himself it couldn't be true. Yet, Cathy kept telling him more and more about how they did the killings, going into greater detail.

"I must have really loved Gwen," Cathy said, "to do that for her."

"How could you do it?"

"Well, those people were probably better off dead."

After months of her story coming out in drips and drabs, punctuated by episodes of anger, rage, and violence, Ken admitted to himself what he knew had to be true.

His wife and Gwen had killed six people. What as worse, if that was possible was that they had not done it because they believed the women would be better off dead.

Cathy and Gwen had murdered because they figured out a way to get away with it. And what was worse, was that they had killed half-a-dozen people because they thought it was fun.

Cathy told him they had wild sex after each killing. As incredible as that sounded, he believed her.

He thought again about how Cathy and Gwen could be together. Why shouldn't Ken think these two women could kill as often as they wanted? After all, they had tried to kill him and would have, if it hadn't been for the intervention of a Grand Rapids police officer.

Still, even after all that Cathy had put him through, Ken had resisted doing what he knew had to be done. He didn't want to turn his wife into the authorities, but Ken knew he should.

Finally, Cathy's stories had worn him down. Or maybe it was her hot-and-cold, bipolar emotional roller coaster he rode with her during those months that showed Ken it was more than possible that his wife had actually done it, that she had really killed people.

He knew it was time.

Ken had to go to the police and tell the story that he had

come to believe was true.

His wife was a serial killer. And if she wasn't stopped, Cathy could kill again.

CHAPTER SEVEN

Since Alpine Manor was in the city of Walker, on the northwest border of Grand Rapids, Ken went to that municipality's police department to tell his story.

The detective who was called away from a quiet Sunday evening at home to talk to him after Ken told his story to the desk sergeant didn't believe Ken anymore readily than Ken had felt Cathy was telling the truth

After all, why should he?

Every one of the people Ken claimed Cathy and Gwen had killed — and he always stressed the murders were Gwen's idea, not his wife's — had died of natural causes. No one had ever raised any red flags or had any suspicions of foul play, at least none worth talking about in those cases, so why be concerned now?

More importantly, why believe Cathy?

The paperwork had been processed. The bodies were buried in the ground. Their families had grieved and moved on.

Why should any of these cases be re-opened?

In fact, Ken Wood was not the most reliable person. His story of what Cathy had told him and how he had reacted was full of holes.

It would have been easy to ignore him, but Detective Tom Freeman did not.

The next morning Freeman went to Alpine Manor to get

Cathy and bring her back to Walker Police headquarters for a conversation.

At first, Cathy told the detective that Ken had made up the story to get back at her. But Freeman told Cathy that he believed Ken and that he didn't think it was the "big joke" that she said it was. He also explained a search warrant had been served at Alpine Manor for medical records, Cathy paused, looked him in the eye, and confessed.

She told Freeman essentially the same story she had told Ken. Cathy talked in graphic, explicit detail about how Gwen had used a rolled up washcloth to kill each of their victims, and how she had stood watch outside the patients' rooms when it happened.

Above all Cathy made it clear to Freeman, that while she wasn't entirely innocent, the murders were all Gwen's doing.

Cathy talked so fast that Freeman had trouble writing it all down. She didn't spare any details. Her mind leaped from patient to patient, from murder to murder.

Sometimes she would compare the way different victims died, telling Freeman who fought back and who submitted.

Cathy told him the story of each and every murder.

She talked about having sex to celebrate, about how Gwen thought it was fun to kill the women, and most of all, how it was all Gwen's idea.

And there was more, Cathy said. She had evidence. She had kept their love letters in which their murder plot, the idea of killing someone for each of the letters in the word "murder" was conceived.

Cathy showed Freeman her poem, Forever and Five Days, which she told him was the motivation for the killings after Gwen's plan -- yes, she said it was Gwen's plan -- to build a blood soaked acronym failed.

Cathy accepted a deal. She would plead guilty to a charge of second-degree murder and go to prison for between twenty and forty years. Her only request was that she not be sent to the same facility as Gwen.

Most importantly, Cathy agreed to break the pledge that she and Gwen had made to never tell on each other.

She would testify against Gwen at her trial.

Gwen was arrested and extradited from Texas. Ironically, she had also confessed. Gwen told Robin about the murders but said the killings had all been Cathy's idea, and that Cathy had actually suffocated the six victims.

Unlike Ken, Robin never believed the story. Even though she had seen Gwen in enough fistfights to know she could handle herself, Robin didn't think Gwen was capable of murder.

Robin was sure Gwen was just making up a crazy story to amuse the both of them. So, she never told a soul.

Gwen related her story to a Kent County, Mich. jury. She didn't deny taking part in the murders, but Gwen said the killings had been Cathy's idea, not hers, and that Cathy had been the one who snuffed out five lives.

She testified that Cathy was always making up stories and spreading rumors and lies. Gwen said she always thought the alleged murder plot was just one of the "head games" that Cathy played, and she went along with it.

"At first it was a joke," Gwen said.

Gwen said she left Cathy for another lover because she "was tired of playing games and hurting people. The games just got out of hand."

Gwen also told the jury that Cathy's confession and decision to implicate her was only an attempt to get back at her for leaving Grand Rapids with Robin Fielder.

Gwen said she realized when she left Grand Rapids that Cathy was angry and "was going to get even, just like she said she was."

Hard as it is to believe that a petite woman like Gwen could have bossed around a 300-pound woman like Cathy and dominated her to the point of murder, the jury bought it.

They decided that Cathy was telling the truth, that she had only taken part in the murders because she wanted to please Gwen.

The only person who spoke in Gwen's defense, was Fran, the woman she had followed to Grand Rapids from Texas. Not a single member of Gwen's family showed up at the trial to lend her support.

"This is not some kind of referendum on homosexuality or lesbianism," Assistant Kent County Prosecutor David Schieber told the jury in his closing argument. "This is not an example of a typical gay relationship. The dynamics of this relationship were destructive -- almost cancerous."

He also said Gwen may not have known the reason for the murders and admitted it was hard to understand how she and Wood could have killed these people.

But in the end, Schieber said their motive was shockingly simple.

"It was just murder for murder's sake," Schieber said. "The motive was intensely personal."

The jury of nine women and three men deliberated for thirty minutes the first day they got the case and about six hours their second day behind closed doors.

Other than Fran Shadden, the woman she followed to Grand Rapids, and the lawyer standing by her side, Gwen was completely alone when she was found guilty of killing five elderly Alpine Manor patients and sentenced to prison for life without the possibly of parole.

Fran was also the only person to speak in Gwen's defense after the verdict was read and the young Texan was taken away to prison.

Fran went into a phone booth to call Gwen's family in Texas and tell them of the verdict, and then emerged to speak to reporters.

Fran said she couldn't believe Gwen had killed anyone and pointed out that no medical evidence of murder was ever found.

It is a fact that a medical examiner who performed autopsies on two of the bodies after they were exhumed from their graves could find no evidence to either substantiate or refute Cathy's story that they had been smothered to death.

"I'm shocked," Fran said. "I don't understand how she could be convicted with no evidence ... just on here-say."

And besides, she said, "Gwen may be capable of a lot of things, but not murder."

FOREVER AND FIVE DAYS

I love you Gwen
I think you're great
For this afternoon
I can not wait

That's when we'll wake and
That's when I'll kiss you.

That's when I'll hold you
Oh Gwen I miss you.

Bunny hop
Over here
And let me lick you
On the ear.

I want to get married
Right now right away
Don't make me wait
Till the day.

When you'r mine
Oh please say
You'll be mine

Forever and five days.

— Cathy Wood

ABOUT THE AUTHOR

Rod Kackley

It's all about the story, as far as Rod Kackley is concerned.

Whether it's Shocking True Crime Stories or one of his many works of fiction. Rod wants to keep you turning pages and reading incredible tales of criminals, their victims, and their capture.

Spoiler alert: No matter how long it takes, the bad guys rarely win. But it's the criminal who is often the most compelling character.

That's true whether it's "Mommy Deadliest," the story of a woman who kills one of her children each time she gets into a fight with her husband, or "The Murder of Thora Chamberlain," the story of a teenage girl and her kidnapper.

In Rod's world of fiction, he spins yarns about "The Coffee Shoppe Killer, a woman who kills her lovers when they disappoint her.

A teenage girl wraps a serial killer around her finger in "Go Big or Go Dead."

Then there's "The Murder of Emma Brown," where two young women go out to party one night, and one only returns home.

Written in Kalamazoo, Michigan, Rod's books and stories allow his readers to brush up against the world of crime without getting hurt.

And it's a heck of a ride!

For more go to rodkackley.com

BOOKS BY THIS AUTHOR

The Murder Of Thora Chamberlain: A Shocking True Crime Story

Mommy Deadliest: A Shocking True Crime Story Of A Murdering Mother

The Iowa Murders: A Shocking True Crime Story

88 Days: The Abduction Of Jayme Closs

The Day Eva Dugan Died: A Shocking True Crime Story

The Murder Of Vanessa Maccormack: A Shocking True Crime Story

#Justice For Ashley: A Shocking True Crime

Story

Never Forgive Never Forget: A Shocking True Crime Story

Murder's Always Murder: Shocking True Crime Stories

Kalamazoo's Suitcase Killer: A Shocking True Crime Story

Sleeping With The Devil: A Shocking True Crime Story

She Deserved Better: A Shocking True Crime Story

She Cries Alone: A Shocking True Crime Story

Murder Is Best Served Bloody

The Murder Of Emma Brown

Never Again: An Internet Killer Thriller

The Coffee Shoppe Killer: Inspired By A Shocking True Crime Story

Go Big Or Go Dead: A Serial Killer Thriller

Empty Minute: A Murder Mystery

Wake The Dead: A Paranormal Mystery

Made in the USA
Monee, IL
08 July 2026

56551302R00027